THIS WALKER BOOK BELONGS TO:

_____

_____

_____

_____

There are **seventeen** kinds of penguin,
but the Emperor is the only one that breeds in
Antarctica in midwinter. The adults arrive at their
breeding areas — often as far as 200 kilometres
from the open sea — in late autumn. A few weeks
later the female lays her single egg and returns to
the sea, leaving the male to keep the egg warm
until it hatches a couple of months later.

At first the male and female take turns to look
after the chick. But soon it is big enough
to be left while both parents go fishing for
its food in the sea. By the time it's
four months old, the young penguin's coat of
fluffy down has been replaced by adult feathers.
It now also sets off for the sea,
where it has to start looking after itself.

For James, John, Steve, Tim and Tony —
and all the other dads
M.J.

For Mum and Dad,
from egg number one!
J.C.

First published 1999 by Walker Books Ltd
87 Vauxhall Walk, London SE11 5HJ

This edition published 2001

4 6 8 10 9 7 5

Text © 1999 Martin Jenkins
Illustrations © 1999 Jane Chapman

This book has been typeset in Humana

Printed in China

British Library Cataloguing in Publication Data:
a catalogue record for this book is
available from the British Library

ISBN 0-7445-8221-0

www.walkerbooks.co.uk

The Emperor's Egg

Martin Jenkins

illustrated by Jane Chapman

WALKER BOOKS
AND SUBSIDIARIES
LONDON • BOSTON • SYDNEY

Down at the very bottom of the world, there's a huge island that's almost completely covered in snow and ice. It's called Antarctica, and it's the coldest, windiest place on Earth.

Antarctica

The weather's bad enough there in summer, but in winter it's really horrible.

It's hard to imagine anything actually living there.

But wait...
what's that shape over there?
It can't be.

Yes!

It's a penguin!

It's not just any old penguin either.
It's a male Emperor penguin
(the biggest penguin in the world),
and he's doing a Very Important Job.

He's looking after his egg.

Male Emperor penguins are about 1.3 metres tall.

The females are a little smaller.

He didn't lay it himself, of course.

His mate did that
a few weeks ago.

But very soon
afterwards
she turned round
and waddled off
to the sea.

That's where female Emperor penguins
spend most of the winter — swimming about,
getting as fat as they can
eating as much as they can,
and generally having a very nice time
(as far as you can tell)!

Emperor penguins mainly eat fish, squid,
and tiny shrimplike animals called krill.

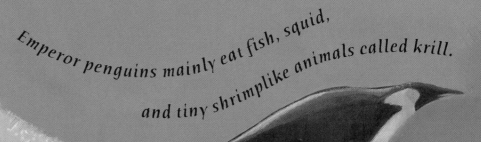

Which leaves
the father penguin
stuck on the ice with
his egg.

Now the most important
thing about egg-sitting is
stopping your egg from
getting cold.

Inside the egg, a penguin chick is starting to grow.

If the egg gets cold, the chick will die.

That means it has
to be kept off the ice
and out of the wind.

And what better
way to do that than
to rest it on your feet
and tuck it right up
under your tummy?

Which is just what the father penguin does.

And that's how he'll stay for two whole months,
until his egg is ready to hatch.

Can you imagine it?
Standing around in the freezing cold
with an egg on your feet
for **two whole** months?

Female Emperor penguins lay one egg in May or June
(which is the beginning of winter in Antarctica).

What's more, there's nothing for
the father penguin to eat on land.

So that means two whole months
with an egg on your feet
and no supper!

I don't know about you

And because he's egg-sitting,
he can't go off to the sea to feed.

Or breakfast   or lunch   or tea.

but I'd be **very very** miserable.

Luckily, the penguins don't seem to mind
too much. They've got thick feathers and lots
of fat under their skin to help keep them warm.

And when it gets really cold and
windy, they all snuggle up together
and shuffle over the ice in a great big huddle.

Most of the time the huddle trundles along
very very slowly.

But **sometimes,**
when the penguins get to a particularly slippery slope ...

they slide down it on their tummies,
pushing themselves along
with their flippers,
always remembering
to take care of their egg —
and trying hard not to bump into each other.

Even though the males keep the egg tucked right up under their tummies when they slide, it sometimes rolls out and breaks.

And that's how the father penguin spends the winter.

Until one day he hears a chip, chip, chip.

His egg is starting to hatch.
It takes a day or so, but finally the egg
cracks right open —

and out pops a penguin chick.

Now the father penguin
has two jobs to do.
He has to keep
the chick warm

and he has to feed it.

*The chick is only about 15 centimetres tall at first,
and much too small to keep warm by itself.*

But on what? The chick is too small to be taken off to sea to catch food, and it can't be left behind on the ice.

Well, deep down in the father penguin's throat there's a pouch where he makes something rather like milk. And that's what he feeds to his hungry chick.

The father penguin can only make enough milky
stuff to feed his chick for a couple of weeks.
But just as he's about to run out,
a dot appears on the horizon.

It gets closer
and closer
and yes!

It's mum!

She starts trumpeting "hello"
and the father penguin
starts trumpeting "hello"
and the chick whistles.

The racket goes on for hours
and it really does sound as if they're
incredibly pleased to see each other.

Every adult penguin has its own special call, like a fingerprint.

Chicks have their own special whistle, too.

As soon as things have calmed down, the mother penguin is sick — right into her chick's mouth!

Yuk,

you may think.

Yum,

thinks the chick.

And it gobbles the lot down.

It's the mother's turn to look after the chick now, while the father sets off to sea for a well-earned meal of his own.

About time too!

INDEX

Look up the pages to find out about all these penguin things.
Don't forget to look at both kinds of word — **this kind** and *this kind.*

ABOUT THE AUTHOR

Martin Jenkins hates cold weather and so has
boundless admiration for Emperor penguin dads.
He isn't a father himself, but he's an uncle
and godfather many times over.
Martin is a conservation biologist, who works for
agencies such as the World Wide Fund for Nature.
He is also the author of **Fly Traps! Plants
That Bite Back** and **Chameleons Are Cool**.

ABOUT THE ILLUSTRATOR

Jane Chapman has wanted to paint pictures of
penguins ever since her honeymoon in 1994,
when she visited a Scottish zoo and saw penguins
waddling along on parade. Jane's other books
for Walker include **One Duck Stuck**
by Phyllis Root and **Where's My Egg?**
by Tony Mitton.

NOTES FOR TEACHERS

The READ AND WONDER series is an innovative and versatile resource for reading, thinking and discovery. Each book invites children to become excited about a topic, see how varied information books can be, and want to find out more.

Reading aloud The story form makes these books ideal for reading aloud – in their own right or as part of a cross-curricular topic, to a child or to a whole class. After you've introduced children to the books in this way, they can revisit and enjoy them again and again.

Shared reading Big Book editions are available for several titles, so children can read along, discuss the topic, and comment on the different ways information is presented – to wonder together.

Group and guided reading Children need to experience a range of reading materials. Information books like these help develop the skills of reading to learn, as part of learning to read. With the support of a reading group, children can become confident, flexible readers.

Paired reading It's fun to take turns to read the information in the main text or captions. With a partner, children can explore the pages to satisfy their curiosity and build their understanding.

Individual reading These books can be read for interest and pleasure by children at home and in school.

Research Once children have been introduced to these books through reading aloud, they can use them for independent or group research, as part of a curricular topic.

Children's own writing You can offer these books as strong models for children's own information writing. They can record their observations and findings about a topic, make field notes and sketches, and add extra snippets of information for the reader.

Above all, Read and Wonders are to be enjoyed, and encourage children to develop a lasting curiosity about the world they live in.

Sue Ellis, Centre for Language in Primary Education